Blastoff! Readers are carefully developed by literacy experts to build reading stamina and move students toward fluency by combining standards-based content with developmentally appropriate text.

Level 1 provides the most support through repetition of high-frequency words, light text, predictable sentence patterns, and strong visual support.

Level 2 offers early readers a bit more challenge through varied sentences, increased text load, and text-supportive special features.

Level 3 advances early-fluent readers toward fluency through increased text load, less reliance on photos, advancing concepts, longer sentences, and more complex special features.

★ **Blastoff! Universe**

This edition first published in 2026 by Bellwether Media, Inc.

No part of this publication may be reproduced in whole or in part without written permission of the publisher. For information regarding permission, write to Bellwether Media, Inc., Attention: Permissions Department, 3500 American Blvd W, Suite 150, Bloomington, MN 55431.

Library of Congress Cataloging-in-Publication Data

LC record for Spanish available at: https://lccn.loc.gov/2025018617

Text copyright © 2026 by Bellwether Media, Inc. BLASTOFF! READERS and associated logos are trademarks and/or registered trademarks of Bellwether Media, Inc. Bellwether Media is a division of FlutterBee Education Group.

Editor: Suzane Nguyen   Designer: Andrea Schneider

Printed in the United States of America, North Mankato, MN.

perro

Table of Contents

¡Hola!	4
At Home	8
At School	12
Por La Tarde	16
¡Buenas Noches!	20
Glossary	22
To Learn More	23
Index	24

¡Hola!

¡Hola! Me llamo Ana.
I speak Spanish,
or *español*.
We can learn
palabras together!

hola (OH-la)
hello

Words to Know

- me llamo (may YAH-moh) .... my name is
- español (ess-pan-YOL) .... Spanish
- palabras (pah-LAH-brahs) .... words
- por favor (POHR fah-VOR) .... please
- de nada (day NAH-dah) .. you're welcome
- perdón (pair-DOHN) .... excuse me

Many **cultures** speak Spanish. People speak Spanish in Spain, **Latin America**, and Equatorial Guinea.

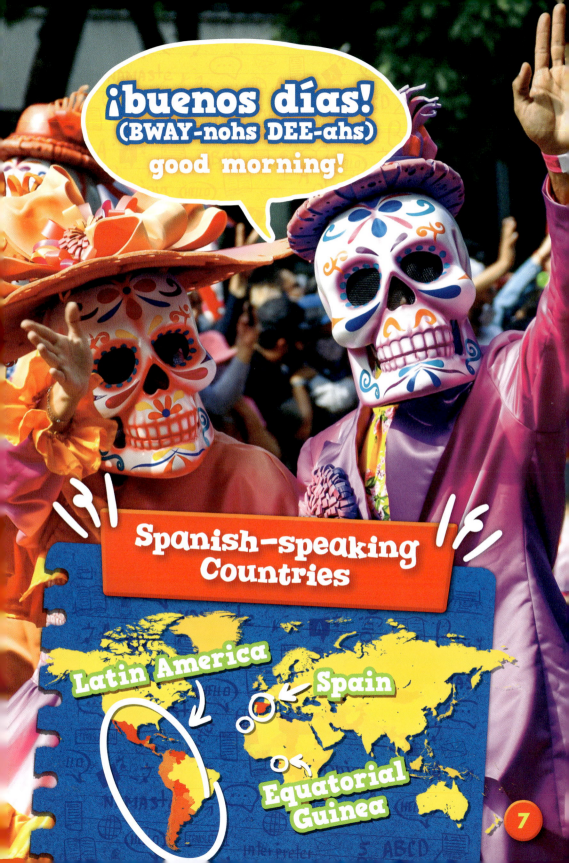

At Home

Lucas lives with his *familia*. He has a *gato*, too!

gato

Words to Know

- familia (fah-MEE-lee-ah).............family
- madre (MAH-dray) ....mother
- padre (PAH-dray) ....father
- casa (CAH-sah) ....house
- perro (PEHR-roh) ....dog
- gato (GAH-toh) ....cat

familia

Daniel gets ready in the *baño* each *mañana*.

espejo

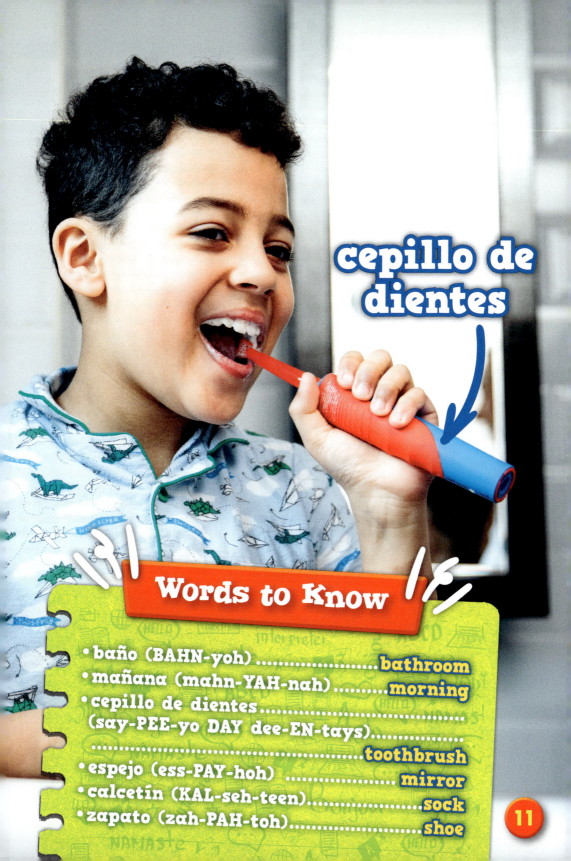

cepillo de dientes

Words to Know

- baño (BAHN-yoh) .... bathroom
- mañana (mahn-YAH-nah) .... morning
- cepillo de dientes ....
  (say-PEE-yo DAY dee-EN-tays)..................
  .... toothbrush
- espejo (ess-PAY-hoh) .... mirror
- calcetín (KAL-seh-teen)....................sock
- zapato (zah-PAH-toh)........................shoe

At School

Sofia walks to her *escuela*. It is time to learn!

lápiz

Count in Spanish

uno (OOH-noh)......1
dos (dohs).................2
tres (trehs)............3
cuatro (KWAH-troh)..4
cinco (SIN-coh)....5
seis (sayis)...............6
siete (si-ET-tay)..7
ocho (OH-cho).............8
nueve (noo-WAY-vay)........9
diez (DEE-ehz)..........10

Words to Know

- escuela (ess-CWAY-lah) .... school
- maestro (my-AY-stroh) ... teacher (male)
- maestra (my-AY-strah) teacher (female)
- aula (OW-lah).......................... classroom
- pupitre (poo-PEE-tray) .... desk
- lápiz (LAH-peez)......................... pencil

David sits with his *amiga* for *almuerzo*. He sips a sweet **horchata**.

Words to Know

- amigo (ah-MEE-goh) .... friend (male)
- amiga (ah-MEE-gah) ...... friend (female)
- almuerzo (ahl-MWAIR-zoh) .... lunch
- comida (coh-MEE-dah) .... food

amiga
amigo

comida

Por La Tarde

Por la tarde, Marta plays *fútbol* with her *hermano*.

María's *madre* makes *cena* for the *familia*. The fried **plantains** are María's favorite!

fried plantains

Words to Know

- cena (SAY-nah).................................. dinner
- plato (PLAH-toh).............................. plate
- tenedor (ten-eh-DOHR).................. fork
- cuchara (coo-CHAR-ah).................. spoon
- cuchillo (coo-CHI-yoh)................... knife
- vaso (VAH-soh)........................ drinking glass

¡Buenas Noches!

Time for bed! Carlos climbs into his *cama*. *Gracias* for a fun *día*!

Glossary

cultures

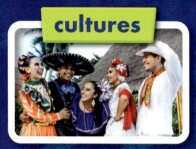

groups that have similar beliefs and ways of life

Latin America

parts of North and South America that speak similar languages

horchata

a creamy, cinnamon-flavored drink often made from rice

plantains

fruits that are like bananas

To Learn More

AT THE LIBRARY

Colley, Jorja. *Cali's Fun Bilingual Tales*. New York, N.Y.: Z Kids, 2024.

Davies, Monika. *Mexico*. Minneapolis, Minn.: Bellwether Media, 2023.

Rosetta Stone. *Rosetta Stone Spanish Picture Dictionary*. Arlington, Va.: Rosetta Stone, 2023.

ON THE WEB

FACTSURFER

Factsurfer.com gives you a safe, fun way to find more information.

1. Go to www.factsurfer.com.

2. Enter "Spanish" into the search box and click 🔍.

3. Select your book cover to see a list of related content.

Index

bed, 20
count in Spanish, 13
cultures, 6
Equatorial Guinea, 6
family, 8, 16, 18
food, 14
good morning, 7
good night, 21
hello, 5
home, 8, 10
horchata, 14
Latin America, 6

learn, 4, 12
map, 7
plantains, 18
play, 16
school, 12
Spain, 6
walks, 12
words to know, 5, 9, 11, 13, 15, 17, 19, 21

The images in this book are reproduced through the courtesy of: NDAB Creativity, front cover; Jne Valokuvaus, p. 3; Andy Dean Photography, pp. 4-5; eve orea, pp. 6-7; Lucas, p. 8 (gato); FG Trade Latin, pp. 8-9; PotPixel, p. 10 (espejo); DGLimages, pp. 10-11; Vitaly Zorkin, p. 12 (lápiz); bluecinema, pp. 12-13; Dayal Guru, p. 14 (horchata); micromonkey, pp. 14-15; PhotoInc, pp. 16-17; Anamaria Mejia, p. 18 (fried plantains); Marcos, pp. 18-19, 22 (cultures); dimamoroz, p. 20 (cama); RenataOs, pp. 20-21; Elena, p. 22 (horchata); Libin Jose, p. 22 (Latin America); Ildi Papp, p. 22 (plantains).